IN 100 WORDS OR LESS...

*+ that may be
too many !*

All my love,

James Wood was born and grew up in Surrey Hills and has been writing for as long as he can remember. A keen jazz musician, James often finds release in poetry and music and frequently performs both in and around York and his home town – most notably, he is a regular performer at York's *Poetry and Pints* evenings. James' perspective on existence and poetry makes him label himself as a failure of a 21st Century beatnik. Whether it is the century or the beatnik in him that is failing him he is yet to discover.

James finds inspiration staring blankly out of his window, and watching films, taunted by the black blinking cursor. He avidly devours other poets' works and also enjoys reading them.

Despite once spending months travelling through Siberia with Mongolian nomads in the Ural Mountains he has never found the burial site of Genghis Kahn. This is his first collection. He is currently studying Literature at the University of York and working on other collections: *Words on Pages* and *Poems You've Read Before, But Worse* and with *Slightly Different Words*.

IN 100 WORDS OR LESS...

James Wood

IN 100 WORDS OR LESS...

Olympia Publishers
London

www.olympiapublishers.com
OLYMPIA PAPERBACK EDITION

A CIP catalogue record for this title is
available from the British Library.

ISBN: 978-1-84897-336-7

(Olympia Publishers is part of Ashwell Publishing Ltd)

First Published in 2013

Olympia Publishers
60 Cannon Street
London
EC4N 6NP

Printed in Great Britain

Dedication

With thanks to MGP and VJM for their support.

Pariter feremus quidquid erit

Ovid.

Acknowledgement

With thanks to *Quirks and Remnants, Alumni* and all those who support me.

Contents

Part I

In 100 Words or Less

...Describe the Benefits of a Community Neighbourhood Watch Program

The meeting started in its usual way:
Two fifteen – on the third Sunday.

I say two fifteen, it was more like
Two seventeen.
Vera was late.

A big one, this week.
It was time, they said
For action.

So we had our tea,
And chats
Of the new building at Shepperton,
Mable's little brats,
the flower show,
the dates of the panto,
the state of that Ethel cow,
the fire at the mill,
how we would probably kill
the fucks that did it,
the hideous new Afrikaans ilk, and
Excuse me, dear,
Could you pass the milk?

…Explore the Socio-Economic Impact of a Capitalist System on the Direct Environment

"There used to be trees here," he said idly
As he took a drag of his cigarette.
I didn't know him;
We were just united by a bus stop.
I smiled politely and shuffled away.

…Explain how Melodious Birds sing Madrigals (Song of the Shepherd)

I feel asleep at the wheel once.
Woke up a half hour later,
In a ditch;
The engine still ticking over.

I got out and wandered 'round a bit.
Had a piss.
There was no one around.
It was glorious.

"It felt as if I was looking at a faded photograph
whose sepia edges encased the smiling faces of its
subjects and held them still, forever. There you are, on the left,
looking down upon the brown water and reminiscing; I
stand beside you, staring at the sky, in protest. Is this not
why we exist? To find old photographs and eternity?"

I had not noticed she had already
fallen into sleep. I kissed her aged hand
and wordlessly left her sanitised room,
with a photograph still in my pocket.

…Explain how Children are too Young to Understand

'What if,' a child once said to me,
As if content to shake the branches of a faded dream
And set me in a reverie:
'All you ever see and touch,
'Amounts to little more than dust?'

Before an answer crossed my lips,
He had long gone to idly dance and play with other kids;
Left me staring at life in bits.
I, astounded by his wit,
Thought: "He's just young. The little git."

...Explore how Modern Ideas of Exponential Expansion Impact 19th Century Romantic Ideals

Further up the road, Blake's Jerusalem,
A beauteous Eden, is dissected
By the A327. A detached
Incision; a vivisection through all
Capability's wonders.

...Pretend to Understand a Complex Japanese Art-form

I
A solitary
White rose, ever slowly growing:
Brings its wild ecstasy.

II
An overbearing
Wall of wood can block
All but the truest light.

Part II: *Summer's Eve*
Debussy's dead leaves,
like ambiguous Death, swirl
around my wine glass.

Part III: *Breaking the Rules*
No one really knows
how to write a real haiku,
but here's one. I think.

Genesis 3: 19

The End
          Hard

fought battles of Ancient Empires

      curl

                  twist

    dance through the air

        settle.

the second

            Drops.

...Hylomorphism

A spider crawled across your floor that night
      and stopped you by the door
It was the first time we had spoken but
      we could find no rapport
I can't remember what you said; only
      that spider by the door.

It was something like: Please, just forget me
      and streams danced on your face
Again, I search my memory to find
      that small spider in your place.

...Tell the Story of your Youth.

I think my mother once told me
that I should always be organ-
ised.

...The Epitaph

Just after the
graves end in the St Mary's
cemetery there's a giant compost
heap. No one seems to get the irony.

...Imagine how Charles was first told he had Leukaemia

we sat
hands clenched
around the ringed table,
talked things through

it wasn't appropriate
they said
inappropriate
they knew
the table knew
the windows knew
the wind knew

when's appropriate?
away early
lights off at 9 and
tired at 3
too much nothing
filling it
can't be appropriate

too busy with
floating
far
far too much
nothing

haven't the time

…Write a Poem about Love

I have no Fanny Brawne, no more.
An obscure Dark Lady;
No Curwen, no Ross, no Dolan,
No Gamble, nor no Lamb
To haunt me and assuage my head.

August ruby held so close!
It has sunk. Shattered by
Every harshest God-curst song of
Moribund angels! No
Neutral tones give me strength to die;

I am left stood in Twickenham
Gardens, content to watch
As others fall to saprophytic
Sorrow, while half-told truths
And lies dance and entwine themselves

Into the hearts of doomèd schemes
With time for revisions,
As indecisions, unspoken,
Obdurately rot and
Putrefy all pure heart-filled vows.

...Explain how the Soothsayers are failing in their Efforts to Convert the Masses

I have always been amazed,
Whene'er I caught the Weather,
To see that rain is brazen,
And the Sun is our tether.

They speak as if they're gods,
with elemental power,
claiming the sun's a panacea
and we should dread a shower.

Amid great droughts, they've prophesied:
"The Sun's out now," bliss ossified,
"Thank Heavens, no more cursèd rain!
That's all from me, see you again."

…Write a Sonnet

I had heard, before my travels took me from home,
That this enduring figure, sat on his darkened
Step, imagining a grandiose, almighty throne,
Never left, nor breathed, nor spoke. But his eyes…

All colours and strokes of melancholy
Were etched into his face. His languid and
Haunting tone… precise, delicate. Always
Making it seem that there was always so
Much left unsaid. A slow, lingering and
Elusive flicker of a shadow of
What was once joy stole across his brow in
Minute miracles. Seeing me, he rose.
This omnipresent antique traveller

Clasped at my vest and rattled my body as if
He gazed into a half-familiar mirror
With stern, restless, and ferocious eyes. But then he
Only clung to me and sobbed and, beneath the perfect tears,
Palely wept: "Ozymandias, what is become of us?"

...Clarify the Complexities of Quiet Carriage Etiquette

There was a kind-eyed woman
On the train to Stevenage,
Teaching her children to read
As her husband slept.

They struggled with innocence
And clarity with exercises;
She smiled – glowed – with rightful pride.
Still her husband slept.

The little girl danced with joy
And giggled when she was right;
The little boy sat perplexed.
Still the husband slept.

I sat idly watching in
Quiet docility and
Wondered, when it was so loud
How he could have slept.

...On Tranquillity of Mind

'Oh, Charlie,'
I appealed to my cat one soggy evening,
'why is writing so tiresome and hard?'

Upon hearing his name, Charlie
sat up and looked around, as if
I'd accused the Earth of being round,
before going back to licking his balls
and that, I think, said it all.

...Describe the Benefits of Censorship: Part I
(The Sermon)

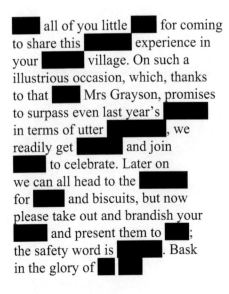 all of you little ▮ for coming
to share this ▮ experience in
your ▮ village. On such a
illustrious occasion, which, thanks
to that ▮ Mrs Grayson, promises
to surpass even last year's ▮
in terms of utter ▮, we
readily get ▮ and join
▮ to celebrate. Later on
we can all head to the ▮
for ▮ and biscuits, but now
please take out and brandish your
▮ and present them to ▮;
the safety word is ▮. Bask
in the glory of ▮

Thanks be to God.

...Describe the Benefits of Censorship: Part II

Letters to the editor regarding the sudden influx of a new concise and obscene art form (1840).

"One day I was reading a limerick,
And the content did make me quite sick.
You see, it was vulgar!
Read one to Aunt Volga
And she beat in my ear with a stick!"

'Dear Sir, your complaint does distress me,
For limericks are the best that they can be,
Ok, so they're rude,
Just don't be a prude;
Please leave all the press and the men be!'

"How dare you, boy, so address me!
Do you know, I could get down and bless thee!
Take it back, you shit
And dumb little git,
Now ban the base form, or so help me!"

… Explain why you think you are the Perfect Candidate for the Trial. (No medical history required.)

I'm sure everyone you know
Has woken up to the rain attacking
Their windows.

It can be unsettling
To hear the barrage of water against
Candid glass.

It can be unsettling
To roll over and feel the expansive,
Cold bed sheets.

I'm sure everyone you know
Has woken up to the rain and wanted
Someone there.

...Empathise with the Plight of Donne's Lovers (White Nights in Russia)

I.

The Sun lingered, saying goodbye to an old friend.

There is a mystic, rare beauty when two
Miracles – Twilight and Dawn – intertwine;
too reluctant to part, even for one
moment. Not heeding the calls of their
mothers, they stay and frolic together.

While I, a mortal, basking in the light,
Watch ice-skaters twirl and dance in the night.

II.

It is 3 A.M.
        Damn this BLOODY
STUPID sun, blaring
        Through these STUPID,
        OBSOLETE curtains!
                Dear Gods, let me sleep!

The childish saplings drowned in an inverted
sea of mist while the remaining Buryats prayed
and tied their cloth to the trees.

                         Beside them a
collection of sacrificed empty bottles
covered their ground, charred by improvised fire.

I simply gazed across the pure, grey waters,
clearer than the honesty of a dying man,
that mercurially licked the wet pebbles
on the shoreline.

                    Elsewhere, Nature's silence was
broken only by the laughter of some drunk,
young man languorously pissing on a rock.

…Postcards (Moving On)

I

No. No, I can't do it,
I simply can't. I've tried
to forget; I've tried to
regret; I've tried every
damned thing to get you out
my head, but still I think
of you and grin and
pick up your pen to write
to you, just one last time.

II

We hadn't spoken for months, but
still I sent you a postcard; full
of all the holiday trite that
postmen know by heart. We hadn't
spoken for months, but I signed it
"I love you." It's still in my desk,
waiting patiently to be sent,
because, let's face it, I still do.

...Poem

My father and I went out
for Chinese, the day I got back,
and only spoke about the chicken
or the weather, or some otiose
shit that neither of us gave a
fuck about.
In each slight,
fucking half-smile that lied its way
through to the facsimiles of two
faces, we buried ourselves into
the stodgy MSG and knew
that she wasn't coming back.

...Advocate the learning of a Poem a Day (Barriers)

I was minding my own business,
queuing up to pay,
for an old copy of some magazine
and Coriolanus,

When some damned lady started talking
about her O levels and the Agincourt speech
in Henry V. She got most of it
wrong, but I feigned a laugh with her
about how time flies.

...Elucidate on why One should Never Trust a Local while Driving a Nice Car

I was ambling home one afternoon,
When some City Type in a saloon
Pulled up beside me and said: 'Good sire,
'Could you please help quell my dear wife's ire?
'You see, my boy, we need direction,
'Anything! Stop her disaffection!'

I had no idea where his destination was,
But said: "Straight ahead, second right – you're not far off."
And so he went, happy as a dog with a bone;
I sauntered on, already late for getting home.
My mother told me never to lie,
Except to those passing City Types.

**...Defend the Idea that if Others had not Beaten You to It,
You'd be Brilliant**

I was going to write a satire
About the pomp of the wealthy,
But then I saw *Made in Chelsea*
And felt robbed of a good idea.

So I thought, 'mocking politics!'
Something dry and yet still witty,
But then I was shown Iannucci
And I openly cursed his antics.

After these trials had been suffered,
I set on a discursive yarn,
But then I went and studied Sterne
And felt that he had it covered...

Last Words

She said to me: "Remember this kiss.
Remember this dance." And she held me.
That was years ago.
She's married now and settled down.
But I can't help but remember that
dance. That kiss. As we span the room around.

She said to me: "Love can't be enough.
Love is never enough." And she laughed.
Or sobbed. I can't say.
She's married now, and settled since.
But still I sit here waiting for her,
thinking always of that slow dance. That kiss.

…Tell the Class what you did during your Holidays. (The Hotel)

I

There is something about hotel rooms
that makes everyone think they're safe;
that they are their true domain and
none can challenge their sovereignty,
even though they are just writhing in
other people's dirty secrets,
re-pressed and packaged for a new
clandestine couple to explore.
A unique, latch-key ideology
that only the maids witness.

II

I'll confess: we were at it
like rabbits in heat
just after we'd checked-in.
Like the rest of mankind
we saw that room as our
domain, our sovereign
land and, like the rest of
mankind – after a long
flight and long looks –
got straight to it.
We checked-in early, at
eleven; they cleaned at
half past.
We shortened our stay.

III

Just like everyone else, they thought the room
was safe for a quick unwind after they'd
arrived. Everyone likes to believe that
no one can hear them sing in the shower.

The Balloon

No one wants to be the Fool at the fountain,
letting the nectar pass his hands.

I had been told myriad times
to write down any ideas; you know,
just in case.
I was idly strolling through town last week,
when a poem started forming in my mind;
all the perfect words in the perfect order
flew into my head and I had a chef-d'oeuvre.
I accosted the passers for a pen and
paper on which to set down my opus,
but…
all I could put down was this…

Part II
Essays

Composure. (The Mysteries of Art)

This here, dear reader, is a poem. You will
know that it is a poem because, no doubt,
you are reading it in some journal called Poems
that deems it worthy. But what's it about?

Is it another dreary poem bemoaning lost
feeling? Or, perhaps, it is a saturnine
song with a catchy refrain that repeats
into its own echoes and leaves you aquiline

to its rhythm, falling gracefully through
the stanzas, dancing with enjambment (or
if you prefer: enjambement) before
striking you with a Nihilistic core?

Perhaps it is about the past. Perhaps
the future. Perhaps the near-present - you know? -
which falls not into either 'past' nor
'future' and is never enough to be Now.

Perhaps it is about all these things
and more. Or less. Perhaps it is just
a poem about nothing at all; filling up a page
or article like a poorly made bike, soon to rust.

Just in case, I suggest you don't
scrutinise it too heavily, but try to let it
speak for itself. Heavens, now it can
speak – how things grow! Soon you'll wit

that it can breathe and flow and have
sex and – oh! But do not worry.
This here, dear reader, is just a poem.

What it's about is mostly up to you. A vague, blurry

and half-blind Poet wrought this out
for you to read and, if they're honest,
to confuse you. Some abstruse critic
may have lauded or spurned it, but promise

that you'll read it and make what
you will of it yourself, because the Writer,
or - if you like it - Poet, has probably
already forgotten all about it.

Attend a Funeral (Eulogy)

If ever there was one true, universal axiom,
"No Regrets" would win through, from the miasmic typeface
                                                and
churning calligraphy of many upper biceps of its drunken,
                                devoted prophets.

But ask your mother, or your father; your brothers,
your sisters, your friends, your neighbours;
your gods of their regrets and a litany will bloom,
all written in fire and stale nostalgia.

From time to time, as the rain laughs through my windows,
I float back to that day: as you counted the waves
and waited for the white sail on the horizon;
still I watch myself stand away, watching you
before you turn, enshrouded by the sea. But still,
I hope you think me of me:
Even fallen leaves create an effortless pattern
To unite one final masterpiece.

A Biography (Derrick 1929-1987)

It was raining as they walked to Sugary Cove,
From deep in the night, the waves came to them faintly.
The sky misted as they said goodbye to love.

She was to leave him, still a stranger,
Taking shelter under the cedar tree.
It was raining as they walked to Sugary Cove.

Talking of things that did not matter,
She was lost in hopeless longing. Slowly
The sky misted as they said goodbye to love.

She thought this chance would be seen by the chronicler,
And how she would weep abundantly.
It was raining as they walked to Sugary Cove.

Saying little, she gazed at the sunless sky; the cover
Of her coat was frayed and she embraced his arm, lovingly.
The sky misted as they said goodbye to love.

With tears matching the waves they held the ether.
The dawn came on, bringing an end to nothing. Gently
It was raining as she walked to Sugary Cove,
The sky misted as she said to goodbye to love.

Tuesday Evening Philosophy (The Thinker/19th April, 19:13)

It yawned into dusk while the weary clouds shivered
And yielded their tears as we hurried along. The
Lit cathedral hovered over the empty fields
With an iridescent, lustrous beauty,

When I caught sight of a solitary figure
Under a distant, leafless oak, gazing up
At the stars, and I marvelled at his life.
It was no masterpiece, and he no master,
But the quiet and the time and place were right;
His Eloquence was greater than speech.

A simple man, contemplating his place under
The cacophony of burning, brilliant
Supernovas in tranquil wonder. I
Longed to approach him, to share in his awe.
We were running late. When I looked back, he was gone.

The Psychosomatic Advantages of Optimism (The Two Brothers)

I

My Mum's been worrying about our neighbour; he's
A kind old man, who says he used to be real cool,
But I don't believe him. On Monday he went out
To walk his dog and came back for it hours later.
He laughs at himself a lot; Mum just sighs.

My Mum says I could learn from him as she watches
Him chuckle to himself if he forgets something,
But I think my teachers wouldn't like it if
I did that. "You know, we have a lot in common,
you and me," he likes to say when we talk.

My Mum says it's sad because his wife went the same
Way, but he's still ok, so she must only be
Hiding and he forgot to find her, or she's
Waiting for him to catch her up so they can hug.
I like our neighbour; I think he's funny.

My Mum says he can't help with my homework, either,
Even though he used to. Our neighbour's really smart.
Yesterday he went out for a walk without his
dog again, but he hasn't come back; I think he
remembered his wife and went to find her.

II

We have this neighbour that went out to walk his dog
and came back for it a half hour later. The one
person not worried about it is him, and he
jokes about setting Easter egg hunts for himself.
We all know that he's terrified, though; you see it
when he cries - late at night - to his wife on his shelf.

Give an Account of Contemporary Existentialist Thought (Sensing)

I am sure that in Hamlet, the Bard expounds on existence,
But … it is very long, and I don't have the persistence.
Certainly, Kant and Nietzsche and Kierkegaard must have
       reams of stuff on life,
But ... it's really rather dry and I thought it not worth the strife.

I had never had a problem,
Thinking and, therefore, being.
True, I have not read the great works
Of Philosophers, all-seeing,
But was really quite content.
And perfectly sure of all things.
Hardly found myself in torment.
Absolutely fine with all life brings.

Except... on one fateful day, an automatic door closed on me,
And now frantic worrying is all I can foresee.
Perhaps…it didn't see me? Or, am I an apparition?!
Now I sit in solitude and fear real life - not perdition.

Ah, memories! (Green Guide)

There they are, on the cover
     having fun and being beautiful

We palmed a lift to the camp in a geriatric cab
with a lost limb; we managed to coax all five of us onto
the back, with Seb riding the four of us and bleeding out where
a door should have been. The stench of the oleaginous
innards of this eviscerated metal frame was stout and
immutable, but we didn't notice it until we found
it buried deep in our clothes. We were focussed on holding
on, for Seb's life. In transit, I glanced a blurry advert and

There they are, on the cover
     having fun and being beautiful,

just like it should be. A too-long whine of agony bought
me back into this echoing carcass and choir of strained and
tense faces, as though we patiently and obediently
awaited torture from some unseen smog. Resigned wheezes
played across the ribs of that flaking cab while Sabine tried to
pollute the air with breath; she struggled for the rest of the trip.
In that haze and under the gaze of those gorgeous people,
I realised that Larkin was not the master, but Titch Thomas.

There they are, on the cover
     having fun and being beautiful.

Agreeable Surprises (Portraits)

Every now and then I realise
That I still have that picture of you
In my wallet. Each time I remind
Myself that I should really take it
Out, but I never do.

It's not on display anymore, but
Tucked away into one end, about
By my cards, like an old trophy
Hidden in a drawer. So, every now
And then, you peek out.

I don't show you around, now, either.
The last time I took you out was at
Lake Baikal, because I know that it
Was a place you had always wanted
To see. We were sat

Behind some old shack as the sun slid
Down to bed behind the mountains. I
Still have that picture of you in my
Wallet. It makes me smile; think of you.
Every now and then.

Evaluate how Sensationalism in the News affects the Perspectives and Sensitivities of a Statistically Ordinary Man's Daily Life (The Commute)

There was a bouquet left by the side of the road,
Some kind of memorial, I think. Flowers, notes;
One had a flag with "We will always love you, Ben"
Written on it. The ink had smudged in the rain
And made it look strange and blurred in my mirrors. Flowers
Were dying, too. It was a strange mausoleum
For him. Death on Display to celebrate life.
I thought it quite funny. A man, just like me,
Going too fast, like me, and topping himself on
A sharp bend, poor bloke. The flowers were replaced a
Few times. Keep the thought of this guy alive, I guess.
Inevitably though, they were just left to die.
The flag was torn, shredded and mocked by the weather.
People always move on. I never knew him, but
I saw him every day.

...Kids These Days...

The problem is: *children don't have any respect anymore.*
                        Overhead at a youth centre.

Monday's child was fair of face,
but lost its looks by the age of eight
Tuesday's child is full of grace,
but is only drawn out through others' disgrace
Wednesday's child is full of woe,
being moved from home to home
Thursday's child has far to go,
and lacks concentration and commitment
Friday's child is a back-talking lout,
who only ever works on its pout.
Saturday's child works on the streets for a living,
having hit the skids with pill addiction
The child that's born on the Sabbath day
Is bonny, blithe, good and gay,
but got abused, bullied, teased and scorned
because it tried. Its parents still mourn.

ziix hacx tiij catax

I'll show you; take my hand

Some people find solace – no, I don't like that, more
like perspective - from science or philosophy
as they whirl around the toilet basin of their
existence, constantly churning against the clock.

I just like to walk. Ever since I was young I
would disappear for a few hours. By myself,
I was a champion, away from the hard truths of
mediocrity; and I would find my own new
Arcadia, selfishly hidden where even
I would never find it again. These portals that
took me to Earth's soul and soil and were open
for only a few glistening moments before
sealing themselves up with sorrowful reticence.

Watch your step on that rock, it doesn't like strangers.

I remember this one time, recently,
I was stepping through a park that I knew
better than anyone can know themselves
and I saw, behind a muted oak tree
and buried under a thick face of leaves,
a timorous stile. Even now I can't
describe where it led. Except, there was this
one, exhausted tree, lying down to rest
and surrounded only by reverent
saplings, metres away. It was an eager
old man with an untamed beard that had just
laid himself down to rest with his loping

arms stretched out behind him – his fingers were
shielding new growth, as they span on the floor.
Except, like when you see a stain of fresh
Bird shit on a gravestone, something had bowled
out the innards of this poor, friendless man,
like a wanker with a melon-baller.
I felt like Augustin in that mansion,
briefly glimpsing Yvonne before losing
himself to an existence of searching.
But never try to get someplace again.

This place, like I say, is the only place
I've ever been able to   find again.
I like it that way. There's a mystery
each time I leave concrete behind, I guess.
It's a bit like Nardis, I think. Well, sort
of. You know it? These lost notes of music,
never really played by the writer or
the commissioner, but picked up by one
unrelated player. But, still, none of
them are important – just those notes. I like
that tune. And, at times like this, engulfed by
my brain and new old friends, it comes to me.
I like the tune. I think it…fits, somehow.
I sit and hum it. And sometimes I talk
to these new old friends that I'll never meet
again, just so they know they're not alone.
I don't like leaving them, either. I guess
I haven't really answered your question.

Itinerary

To wander, blissfully lost, through the moribund
          streets of a deserted town

To lose count, of all the self-made and unenforced
          promises that help you change your life
              but never make it through the night

To appeal, spuriously, to everything that ever was is and will be
          before spiralling up and
             letting time butcher you

To read in the lines and cracks in every
          barren face and soaked sepulchre
            the same perpetual and
               inexplicable question

                      of each squirming
yesterday's lovers

To hear the cacophony of joyful wails
          forcefully rent and blended with
            elongated echoes torn from the same
            vocal chords

To arrive, blissfully lost, at an unscheduled stop
          and realise it all seemed to
            work out
              regardless

To wonder, blissfully lost, through the moribund
          streets of a deserted town

Section B: Describe your House. (The Playground)

I don't know when it was, but over the top of the broken,
old and moaning dead fridge that, somehow, found its
grave in my living-room, I watched my quaint, geriatric
neighbour dust the outside of her windows. Between the abyss
of her precariously supported garage – that, I kept telling her,
desperately needed updating – and the rotting window frame,
she perched herself and stretched out her unnourished arm
to wipe the 'sill. Mine are left to the vagaries of the rain.

My beaten-up TV was still smouldering
out its array of ominous blues and greens
when I saw her again, barbarically
hacking at her front lawn. The glowing bleak and incomplete
                                                                    teams
of unfinished crosswords stole space with the wind and verbally
asserted their presence, as if scared of yellowing too far.
I cranked up the volume and tightened my grip on my dear
                                                                    John.

Touch (Advice)

I

Ok, being in love is just like holding hands –
it's a symbol of itself; a microcosm.
You feel warm and close, like everything is just right;
but if you hold too tightly, or never let go
it gets clammy and hot and dirty. So, in time,
stand to face the wind and breathe out faintly: Thank you.

II

Well, when the clock stops and our own traffic lights cease
to control the ebb and flow of our own red sea,
that is when our own sentient metropolis
falls fast to mutiny and riots or, simply,
to calm and compliant rest. That counted time, when
an eternity can feel like nothing at all.

Promote the Notion: "Everyone can Write"
(Show and Tell)

How hard can it be?
All you need to do is put all the words –
those dazzling, heartfelt words – into an
order to make everyone and every eye who peers upon it
smile and weep. All you need to do is
offer yourself up like a
lover's open palm
to the eyes of the whole World.

You will compose these notes into a solitary
letter with no address; a love-song of yearning
to one you shall never meet, but always know.

Like a child in front of the class
you twist your foot and stare
at the ground, the captivating
ground, and try to remember
to breathe and remember
those words. Those sudden, coruscating
words that you grotesquely grind out
to condense existence, and
those teasing, abstract nouns
so perfectly
trapped and caged;
A perfect order with a
neat, clever rhyme
that is effortless – fresh -
inspired.
Those words, those impatient
harlequins, to seize and shackle in perfect place
every wish upon
every wick &

burning oil.
For the whole Class to digest
and in time, perhaps,
to regurgitate, but not in your
perfect order – not the perfect
litany of direction and rhyme –
they'll re-arrange, tear apart and maim your symphony, so
perfectly conceived, into
a conspiracy of vacant words.
Not perfect. Not in order.
A jumbled obfuscation of empty
symbols.

How hard can it be?

Wipe your sweat-flooded hands onto
your trouser leg
when you think,
think the teacher is not looking
and try
try with all your life
try with all your being
try with all your dissidence now soaking in a World of eyes and
expectance
try to remember.

Swallow hard.
How hard can it be?

How hard can it be?

A Poem about Nature (Welcome to Jerusalem; Population: 2, 364,562)

It's the quiet drive home,
Through the bright pallor of
Twilight that flits among the shadows

When you can really see
To what the World comes. The
Haze can lift, leaving beauty's heir.

In the quiet you roam,
And hear melodies of
Passion dance across the dry meadows

And iridescently
Breathing life. A lonely
Moon slowly grows to the quiet sound

Of Nature's ode from beasts;
Creatures that, in the light,
Are repulsed by the gross doctrinaire.

Yet, a mausoleum
Exists throughout the night –
Fulfilling its place in existence.

The pleasant pastures green
Escaped the Dark Mills, but
The smell of petrol hangs in the air.

On the Death of our Esteemed Friend and Colleague.

waiting for light waiting for dawn waiting for warmth waiting
for the pisser waiting
waiting for the toast waiting for the kettle waiting for the tea
waiting for the sink waiting
waiting for the bus waiting for the stop waiting for the train
waiting for the stop waiting
waiting for the tube waiting for the stop waiting for 9 o'clock
waiting for the papers

                            waiting
waiting for the pisser waiting for a drink waiting for the
meeting waiting for the late arrival

                            waiting

waiting for lunch waiting for lunch waiting for the sandwich
maker waiting for his turn

                            waiting

waiting for the kettle waiting for the meeting waiting for the
boss waiting for the punch-line

                            waiting
waiting to stop laughing waiting for business waiting for a pat
on the back waiting for a

            pat on the back waiting
waiting for the computer waiting for I.T. waiting for a drink
waiting until Sarah bends

            slowly over   waiting

75

waiting for 5 waiting for 5 waiting for 5 waiting for 5 waiting
for 5 waiting for 5 waiting
waiting for the tube waiting for the stop waiting for service
waiting for the slow waiting
waiting for the food waiting for dessert waiting for drinks
waiting for the tube waiting
waiting for the stop waiting for service waiting for drinks
waiting for drinks waiting
waiting for that look waiting for that drunken half-smile waiting
for that sign waiting
        for the explosion in the forsaken cubicle that out
shadows existence
        waiting for a cab waiting for her to leave
        waiting for her scent to leave
        waiting for the inevitable tears after the photo-frame
waiting for fatigue waiting for sleep waiting for cold waiting for
dusk waiting for dark
 waiting.

Oneirology

Sometimes, when I'm falling, I don't even think about the pain
but let myself dissolve like a doomed man, malformed into
                                                        water;
and then, as this momentous bead, I allow myself to plummet
                                                with the rain,
before exploding myself into innumerable, minute droplets.

But, as I stare sightlessly at the evolving stars that, like
a neglected fire, sputter and cough themselves in and out of
consciousness, I picture myself falling. I plunge, lost and
                                        obsequious, like
Pilate straining through the tempests of folklore. Comatose, my

command evaporates from me and moist beads amass on my
                                face. This delirium, so hidden
by my own invention, cleaves itself away and leaves solely a
                                hand pawing at the coffin lid.

Part III

Being a Showcase for the Profound work of Benedict S. G. Conners

Daily News
By Benedict S. G. Conners

Fires threaten hundreds in Utah
More die in Helmand
Stocks fall
        fall
            fall
Rwanda
Khmer Rouge
Syrian warfare
Terrorist bombings
9/11
7/7
Wild gunman kills family
Raoul Moat
Banks close
Riots burn
Thousands die after Earthquake
famine
war
disease
and still you don't come back

My Friend Rich has Behavioural Problems
By Benedict S. G. Conners

First:
Thirdly: drunk paralytic on off attempt **sing** *big booty bitchez, I got* sway Macarena under storm lighting NON-STOP Rocky steps tumbling up (parenthesis) – hyphenated at-tack-ack-ck-k + π & and chaNgE SNAP our prices are so low you'l be mad to miss them our prices are so low you'l be mad to miss them our prices are so low you'l be mad to miss them

⸮■♎ ♦♒♋♦▱ ♎♏♒□ ♌□◲▱ ⋇♦ ◲□♦□ ●□♦◱

Visiting hours are 12:00 – 13:00

and what are your thoughts on the 12:15 at Chepstow?

Document 1
By Benedict S. G. Connors

I stared blindly at that white sheet,
while the black cursor blinked out
the tedious seconds, and it taunted me
with its barrenness.
I tried typing; here's what came up:

In that precise moment, just after the doors
have been closed, you can perceptibly hear the
wailing cry of a new-born babe as its very own
hourglass starts leaking gold through all the
cracks in its haunted frame. It is a sinister
onus to tell a child the certain obliquity
in every soundless and despotic hour
that lacks the sun and cries the imperceptible
darkness from its chest, authorizing its limbs -
silently flailing and cowering in acquiescence –
fragment and cry out from its split
peace; then melt, with a sluggish
rapidity, covering the Earth in
chthonic blackening.

It's fine. A bit dreary but
I use some clever words.
I'll keep it up and maybe
give it some obtuse (use that…)
title that'll hold it together

* Buy thesaurus. Internet keeps crashing.